4 Steps to Building Your Brand

BY CHRISTOPH DYER

Copyright © 2018 Dyer Publishing Company.

All rights reserved. This book or any portion thereof may not be reproduced or used in any manner whatsoever without the express written permission of the publisher except for the use of brief quotations in a book review. For permission requests, write to the publisher, addressed "Attention: Permissions Coordinator," at the email address below.

Published by Dyer Publishing Company, in the United States of America.

First printing, 2018.

Dyer Publishing Company

Chicago, IL

www.DyerPublishing.com

info@DyerPublishing.com

CONTENTS

INTRODUCTION 1

STEP 1: ACTION 5

STEP 2: BUILD 25

STEP 3: CREATE 41

STEP 4: DOMINATE 61

ACKNOWLEDGEMENTS 95

ABOUT THE AUTHOR 97

BY CHRISTOPH DYER

INTRODUCTION

AMAZON, MCDONALD'S, DISNEY

These companies have names that instantly bring to mind various thoughts, feelings, and perceptions about the products or services they each provide. Even if you have never ordered a product on the Internet, eaten fast food, or taken a vacation to a kids' theme park, you still know these names because of the strong marketing and advertising efforts by each of these companies.

They are successful because they understand the power of building a brand. Creating a business is one thing, but building it into a brand is something totally different. Branding involves building your business in a different way by following some strategic steps that will make your business into a household name.

This book will provide you with the steps it takes to create a business with the proper legal foundation, as well as how to build a website that looks professional and is user friendly, that will attract new clients to your business without you having to spend tons of money. Next you will learn how to create an effective social media presence on all the top social media sites, which is where your customer is at every day interacting with their friends and family.

Finally, this book will show you how to increase your business customer base by using the Internet to advertise your brand, also known as digital marketing. Digital marketing will allow you to reach large numbers of people that have an interest in your products or services, that are socializing, web surfing, or using phone apps within your area.

The greatest value of this book is that you will learn strategies that will enable you to build your business or idea into a brand name over time without having to spend the millions of dollars that the major brands of your childhood had to spend to be relevant.

DEFINITION OF A BRAND

According to the American Marketing Association dictionary, a brand is a "name, term, design, symbol, or any other feature that identifies one seller's goods or services as being different from those of other sellers." Branding allows a company to set itself apart from the competition by making the consumer believe in the quality and superiority of the brand versus all the other generic products or services available.

According to an article entitled "How Brands Were Born: A Brief History of Modern Marketing" in the TheAtlantic.com, during the middle of the twentieth century, a shift occurred which required companies to find a new way to differentiate themselves from their competitors. These companies began to create advertising messages that demonstrated how the potential buyer should think and feel about what the company was selling.

The advertising was delivered in many ways, such as celebrity endorsements and television, radio, and print ads. Product placement in movies was also very popular; this involved your favorite actor or actress using a product to create an image of a specific lifestyle, mood, or feeling.

You may remember the classic image created by early television of celebrities like Ricky Ricardo constantly lighting up cigarettes, which was meant to make people buy into that cool and classy lifestyle of smoking. Classy is probably the last thing someone thinks of if they have ever been in a closed room with someone smoking cigarettes.

The tobacco industry's branding has worked so well, that even though there has not been a television or radio ad for cigarettes in the United States since 1971, these companies still make billions of dollars every year.

Reading this book will assist you in creating the right image for your growing business, which will help influence how customers view your company and its products. This will involve you making some conscious efforts to set your business apart from the competition by doing what others are not willing to do.

After completing the 4 Steps to Building Your Brand found in this book, you will have the knowledge you need to be successful in every business venture you are involved in.

Please take lots of notes while reading this book, so you can learn as much as possible about the ways to become a profitable business, reach more customers, and advertise your company using digital marketing as well as social media. This book will help you regardless of what type of business you have. Whether you are a cosmetologist, real estate agent, investor, travel agent, store owner, or just a person with a dream, this is the book for you.

Now let's begin the process of taking your brand to the next level using the contents of this book as your guide through the trials and tribulations of the business world. This book is here to help you to avoid making some of the common mistakes that will cause your business to lose money. It will give you the basic understanding you need to effectively advertise and market to the people you want to spend money with you.

FINDING YOUR PATH IN THIS BOOK

This book contains some great information that will allow you to reach your goals in life, but it is important to first do a complete analysis of your business, idea, product, or service. This analysis begins with what seems to be one of the hardest things for most people that have created something—critiquing it—because of the personal attachment that comes with creativity. It is hard for some people to be a critic of something they have created or believe strongly in, even if they know the reality of the situation they are up against.

We all have the ability to think of good business ideas, but it takes a true visionary to be able to break down every aspect of that idea, whether good or bad, in order to gain an advantage over everyone else with that same idea. Take it from the entrepreneur, musician, and visionary Sean "P. Diddy" Combs, who made this powerful comment during the Revolt Music Conference in 2017: "I was a dreamer; I started this whole thing as a dream." He went on to say, "You have to really face the reality of what it's going to take to achieve your dream."

The fact is, being an entrepreneur is hard work, but if you learn to work smarter and not harder, then you will be able to have more success than you have ever dreamed.

Now that you understand what a brand is, why it is important to create a strong one, and the necessity for being objective when you look at your company's brand, let's take a look at the first of the 4 steps to becoming a profitable business: Action.

BY CHRISTOPH DYER

STEP 1: ACTION

In order to do business in this complex world we live in, it is important that you take action by developing a legal business entity. This not only will allow you to benefit from the financial success of your idea, product, or service, but it can also shield your personal finances from the operational issues that may arise. A legal business entity is defined as an association, corporation, partnership, proprietorship, trust, or individual that has legal standing in the eyes of the law.

A legal entity has legal capacity to enter into agreements or contracts, assume obligations, incur and pay debts, sue and be sued in its own right, and be held responsible for its actions. In the United States of America, individual states are responsible for facilitating the registration of legal business entities. In this chapter, we will discuss the most common types of business structures in use today: C corporations, limited liability companies (LLC), partnerships, S corporations, and sole proprietorships. You will also get an overview of the additional steps needed to ensure you have the correct structure in place from day one, so your business has the greatest chance of being successful.

CREATE A LEGAL BUSINESS ENTITY

When deciding which business structure is best for your type of operation, you must ask yourself some key questions. In answering these questions, please pull out a sheet of paper and put some real thought into your answers. These questions are designed to make it easier to complete the articles of incorporation when that time comes later in the process:

1. How many partners do you currently have in this business? (Include yourself.)
2. What state will you be doing business in?
3. What is the purpose of your business? (What is the product or service?)
4. Do you plan to sell shares to outside investors?
   a. This is a very important question because selling shares of your business to outside investors allows you to legitimately raise equity capital for your business, meaning cash from investors that does not need to be paid back versus debt which comes in the form of loans and issuing corporate bonds.
5. Do you want to shield your personal assets from being liable for business debts and obligations? Yes or No
6. Are all owners and investors US citizens? Yes or No
7. Will this business be owned by another business entity or individuals? Yes or No
8. Do you want the option of reporting business profits and losses on personal tax returns? Yes or No
9. Are you able to keep up with corporate filings, annual meetings, and recording meeting minutes? Yes or No

Now that you have answered the questions, let's discuss the common types of business structures used in the United States of America today. Please review the current laws in your state to confirm all legal and tax information contained within this book, because tax policies and laws frequently change, and they can also vary drastically from state to state.

It's always a good idea to consult with a certified public accountant as well as an attorney. You should also review the website for the state you plan to incorporate in for further details on all the types of corporations, fees, and guidelines.

C CORPORATION

This is a very popular type of business structure in the USA because it allows the owners to separate their legal and tax obligations from the business. It also separates the owner's personal assets from being used to pay off business debts and liabilities. C corporations can also have an unlimited number of shareholders, which allows the business to raise unlimited amounts of equity capital through the issuing of shares of stock.

You are required to hold annual meetings as well as record minutes from those meetings and file annual reports with the state. Some people do not like the way C corporations are taxed because the business is taxed on all corporate profits, and then the individual owners are taxed again on their personal income from the company, including dividends.

This is often referred to as double taxation amongst the business community, which leads to lots of spirited political debates about corporate tax reform. But the owners are also allowed to split the profits and losses with the business to lower the overall corporate tax rate of the company.

S CORPORATION

An S corporation is very similar to a C corporation in that it provides an independent legal and tax structure as well separates the owner's assets from that of the business. S corporations are also required to hold annual meetings as well as record minutes from those meetings and file annual reports with the state.

There are two major differences that separate an S corporation from that of its predecessor, which may sway some into this type of business entity. The first difference is the limitations on the ownership within an S corporation, which limits the number of shareholders to one hundred individuals that must be US citizens. S corporations are not allowed to be owned by C corporations, LLCs, partnerships, or other S corporations.

Also with an S corporation the owners report their share of the business profits and losses on their personal tax return, which eliminates the double taxation issues that are inherent with C corporations.

LIMITED LIABILITY COMPANY (LLC)

An LLC provides owners the ability to separate their personal assets from the business's legal obligations and liabilities. Limited liability company owners do not need to file a corporate tax return; instead, they report all profits and losses on their personal tax return, which is very similar to a sole proprietorship or partnership.

An LLC can have an unlimited number of owners but cannot issue shares of stock to potential investors. The owners of an LLC do not have to be US citizens nor are they required to hold annual meetings and record minutes. Lastly, a limited liability company can be owned by a business entity or owned by individuals.

PARTNERSHIP

In a partnership, the partners are personally liable for all lawsuits filed against the business. The partners are also responsible for all business debts and obligations that may arise during the life of the partnership. A partnership may not sell shares of stock in the business. Instead, they may raise capital through adding limited partners that invest in the business but have no management or voting rights. Partnerships can have an unlimited number of owners that do not have to be US citizens, but a partnership is not able to be owned by another business, only individuals. No annual meetings or recording of minutes is required in a partnership. In most states there is no filing or name registration required to form a partnership, which makes it very easy to form one. Lastly, all profits and losses in a partnership are reported on the personal taxes of the owners, so no need for corporate tax filings.

SOLE PROPRIETORSHIP

This is the simplest business structure in the United States because there is only one owner in a sole proprietorship and that owner is fully liable for all debts, liabilities, lawsuits, and obligations of the business. No state filing is required to form a sole proprietorship in most states, which makes it easy to form one. The profits and losses of the business are reported on the owner's personal tax return, and any investments in the business would have to be made in the form of personal loans.

CHART 1.1. BUSINESS ENTITY SPREADSHEET

	C Corp	S Corp	LLC	General Partnership	Sole Proprietor
Owners have limited liability for business debts and obligations	x	x	x		
Created by a state-level registration that usually protects the company name	x	x	x		
Business duration can be perpetual	x	x	x		
May have an unlimited number of owners	x		x	x	
Owners need not be US citizens or residents	x		x	x	x
May be owned by another business, rather than individuals	x		x		
May issue shares of stock to attract investors	x	x			
Owners can report business profit and loss on their tax returns		x	x	x	x
Owners can split profit and loss with the business for a lower overall tax rate	x				
Not required to hold annual meetings or record meeting minutes			x	x	x
Permitted to distribute special allocations, under certain guidelines			x	x	

DETERMINING A NAME FOR YOUR BUSINESS

Now that you are at this step in the process, you should have an idea of what you want to name your business. First you want to conduct a name search on your state's website database in order to make sure the name you have chosen is available within your state of incorporation. Simply go to your state's corporate filing website and conduct a name search to ensure you can register your company under your chosen name.

You should also consider utilizing DBA (doing business as) names. A DBA name will allow you to do business in your state of incorporation under a different name than your corporation name.

In most states it is required that you register all DBA names, and there may be a fee associated with setting up a DBA depending on the state. Lots of companies utilize

DBA names, especially sole proprietors, because it is the simplest way to separate your personal identity from your professional business without having to form a corporation or LLC. It is also required that a sole proprietor have a registered DBA name in order to open bank accounts in the company's name, so that payments directly to the business can be received from clients.

Once you have determined what your company name will be and have checked to make sure it is available within your state, the next step is to register that name with the state. If you have a name or logo that you feel is unique and special to your business, you should consider filing for a federal trademark. A federal trademark will help you define your company's brand in the market without you having to worry about someone trying to duplicate your name and logo in other states throughout the country.

Keep in mind trademark protection alone will not be enough to hinder someone else from duplicating your name and logo, but you have to be able to enforce your trademark through the filing of a lawsuit anytime someone infringes on your trademark. If you don't have the ability or financial means to enforce your trademark, then you run the risk of your company's name and logo becoming commonplace in the market, which would weaken your trademark and severely limit the legal remedies available.

REGISTER YOUR CORPORATION WITH IRS

You are now ready for the next step in the process, which is to obtain your Federal Tax-ID Number, also known as your Federal Employee Identification Number (FEIN). This is a unique nine-digit number assigned to your business by the Internal Revenue Service (IRS). Any business entity operating within the United States needs a FEIN, for the purposes of identifying the business for tax and legal proposes.

For more information on FEINs and how to apply for one, use the link below: www.irs.gov/businesses/small-businesses- self-employed/apply-for-an-employer-identification-number-ein-online

Next, most states require the business to have a registered agent. According to legelzoom.com, a registered agent is a responsible third-party who is registered in the same state in which a business entity was established and who is designated to receive service of process notices, correspondence from the secretary of state, and other official government notifications, usually tax forms and notice of lawsuits, on behalf of the corporation or LLC. The registered agent must be at least eighteen years old, and he or she also must be a naturalized citizen in most states.

Now we are at the final step in the process of building your business foundation, which is to complete the articles of incorporation on your state's website. The following information is required, but luckily you already have all of this written out based on the questions you answered earlier in this chapter. The general questions you need to answer for the articles of incorporation are as follows:
1. The corporation name
2. The name and street address of the registered agent
3. The purpose of the corporation
4. The number of shares the corporation is authorized to issue
5. The names and addresses of the officers within corporation, and their signatures

You have now completed building the foundation for your product, service, or idea, and you are officially a legal business entity. You are now properly prepared to actually market and advertise this business in your state.

You should also set up a business bank account once you receive your articles of incorporation back from the state along with your FEIN. This will allow you to cash the checks written in your business's name, once customers start to purchase your product or service.

It's also suggested that you begin keeping track of all financial transactions with vendors or employees through your business bank account. This makes your life so much easier when it comes time to file taxes for your business, minimizing the need to keep a million receipts filed away.

CONSULT WITH AN ATTORNEY

Now that we have discussed the various types of business entity structures, next you will receive the remainder of the road map needed to have a strong business foundation. That next step on this road toward business success is to consult with an attorney, mainly for the purpose of structuring business contracts between yourself and any partners. The attorney will also guide you in the various types of contracts, licenses, and permits required for your type of business in your state.

This is very crucial because you don't want to spend any money developing your business only to find out later that your state has requirements that will prolong your entry into the market or make it impossible. Or even worse, you don't want your company to look unprofessional because it does not have the proper contracts and agreements in place to conduct legitimate business.

In addition to consulting with an attorney, search the Internet for a business contract software program for your type of industry. Purchasing a program with the contracts you need can save you thousands of dollars over the years as well as increase professionalism amongst clients and colleagues. With most of these software programs, the contracts are general agreements with blank spaces which allow you to input your company information as well as add any additional agreements or terms you want to add.

As laws in your industry change, you can update the agreements yourself to reflect any changes in the marketplace or economic structure of the agreement. You can also pay a lawyer to review your pre-made contracts and agreements to ensure they are rock solid, while saving yourself a little money.

Lawyers are paid based on the time it takes them to complete a task for you, so if they are simply reviewing a document you created with your contract software program, the fees should be less. You may find a lawyer that is not willing to work with you this way, but many will. It never hurts to ask.

CONSULT WITH A CERTIFIED PUBLIC ACCOUNTANT

The next important step is to consult with a certified public accountant (CPA). Taking the time to do so in the early phases of building your business could prove to be very valuable to you as your business starts to grow. A certified public accountant can assist you in understanding the tax laws relevant to your type of company as well as in determining the number of authorized shares to issue in the articles of incorporation. As your business begins to generate money, the accountant can also help you keep the proper records needed for tax filings in later years. The accountant can also help you prepare financial statements needed for potential investors and lenders, such as income statements, balance sheets, and cash flow statements.

Financial statements are extremely important to potential investors because they give a glimpse into the financial inner workings of your business, so the investors can make an informed investment decision. The accuracy, honesty, and integrity of your financial documents are critical to the longevity of your business.

For instance, the cash flow statement, which is also referred to as the statement of cash flows, allows investors to understand how you run your business by showing the flow of cash in and out of your business. The statement of cash flows lets investors and banks know the short-term viability of your business, which is directly correlated to your ability to pay the bills of your business. The cash flow statement specifies where the cash comes from, which is separated into three categories: cash flow from operations, cash from investing, and cash from financing.

Cash flow from operations refers to any cash received from customers for services and/or products minus the cost of goods sold. Cash from investing refers to the purpose or sell-off assets such as land, equipment, and financial securities. Lastly, cash flow from financing refers to any cash that comes into the business from banks, investors, and shareholders, as well as any cash that flows out of the company in the form of dividends, debt payments, and taxes. Get an accountant to help you to understand these things, or do your research before the IRS comes knocking on your door.

RESEARCH PAYROLL COMPANIES

It's always good to utilize a payroll company for paying employees instead of having to personally handle the payroll taxes for each employee. Payroll is a complicated beast because it involves several components which can

be quite confusing to properly understand and calculate. The common components of payroll are as follows:
- Salary or rate of pay
- Federal taxes
- State and local taxes
- Federal Insurance Contributions Act (FICA)
- Federal Unemployment Taxes (FUTA)
- State Unemployment Taxes (SUTA)

Along with the above-mentioned items, there may also be some additional elements to payroll, some of which may be optional depending on your state. These other elements are as follows:
- Workers' compensation
- Health care contributions
- 401(k) or retirement contributions

It is crucial that you consult with a certified public accountant or payroll company in order to understand your state's local tax policies regarding the issuing of payroll. Tax laws change frequently, and you need to be aware of all the expenses and liabilities your company will be exposed to when it hires a new employee. You also need to be aware that the components of payroll can severely impact your company's net income, so you need not bypass this subject; instead, have a full understanding of all the elements of payroll prior to bringing on your first employee.

Once you have all of the legal elements in order, it is time to start setting goals.

SHORT- AND LONG-TERM GOAL ASSESSMENT

Part of taking action is setting goals. Doing so will allow you to define your success so you can take the right action to move toward it. In the next two sections, you will learn two strategies, the SWOT analysis and SMART goal-setting, for assessing and setting goals. These strategies for analyzing your business have been used by millions of successful companies around the world. Once again, please take lots of notes and apply these strategies to each business idea you develop, in order to properly assess the risk you are facing, so you can overcome it.

SWOT ANALYSIS

First let's discuss the SWOT analysis. A SWOT analysis is a strategic planning technique that organizations use to identify the strengths, weaknesses, opportunities, and threats related to the business venture ahead. A SWOT analysis will assist you in properly assessing the real risk associated with your business while paying attention to the things that will make your business a strong and dominant company in the market. The purpose is to identify specific business objectives as well as be honest with yourself about the internal and external factors that could make you either succeed or fail at achieving your objectives.

When completing the SWOT analysis, you ask and answer questions under each topic, being completely honest about every aspect of your business. Strengths and weakness are usually internally related to the people within your business and the products or services you plan to sell, while opportunities and threats are things external to your business that will still affect where and how you do business.

Be as honest as possible because doing so will only help you be better prepared when that weakness or threat arises during the normal course of business. Many companies do not plan to fail; instead, they just fail to plan. This leads to them having to shut down because they were not prepared for the obstacles ahead of them, or even worse, they knew the risk but ignored it. The following is a brief overview of the four components of the SWOT analysis:

STRENGTHS

Things about the business or product that give it an advantage over the competition.

WEAKNESSES

Things about the business or product that give it a disadvantage relative to the competition.

OPPORTUNITIES

Something within the business environment that the business could use to its advantage to get ahead of others.

THREATS

Any element of the business environment that could interfere or cause trouble

You can use the questions in chart 1.2 below when doing your own SWOT analysis:

CHART 1.2. SWOT ANALYSIS CHECKLISTS

	Favorable	Unfavorable
Internal	**Strengths** 1. What are the strengths of your brand? 2. What do you do better than everyone else? 3. What are the unique characteristics of your products or services? 4. What additional resources do you have that others do not? 5. What do customers love about your products?	**Weaknesses** 1. What is your business not good at? 2. What are your competitors better at than you? 3. What can your brand improve or do better? 4. What do your customers dislike about your products?
External	**Opportunities** 1. What outside factors will have a positive impact on your business? 2. What favorable economic factors exist? 3. What consumer needs do you meet that competitors do not?	**Threats** 1. What conditions exist that may negatively impact your brand? 2. Is your staff ready for the new initiatives? 3. Will your vendors be able to keep up with growing demand?

BY CHRISTOPH DYER

SMART STRATEGY

Now that you understand the SWOT analysis, let's take a look at the second goal-setting strategy, the SMART strategy. In order to be successful in business, you must have some clearly defined goals with specific objectives in mind. Simply saying you want to get more customers or make more money sounds great, but in reality those are very vague statements that have no real meaning without you attaching actual plans and time commitments to them. SMART is an acronym used by many corporate CEOs and business professionals for creating actionable business goals. The strategy is to create goals that are specific, measurable, achievable, realistic, and time based. Using a SMART strategy helps the business stay on track when goal setting by making sure they adhere to basic business principles of success.

This strategy also enables owners of a company to create a credible vision for the future that can be used in business plans, executive summaries, etc. Let's review each topic within the SMART strategy which will help create the road map needed to be successful in all you do moving forward. Take out some paper and take notes in this section about your business in relation to each one of these topics.

SPECIFIC

The goal should be focused and well defined. For example, "We will open ten new stores within Metro Atlanta," sounds much better when motivating your employees than, "We are going to expand everywhere." By focusing the goal on something specific, you create power versus ambiguity. You show that you are setting realistic goals versus being overly ambitious but with no real plan. So be very specific about what you want to achieve by drilling down deep into the motivating factors behind your vision. Do not leave out anything.

MEASURABLE

Your goal must be quantifiable, meaning there must be some numbers and financial goals associated with the idea for the business to be able to track the progress. This could be as simple as the above statement of, "We will open ten new stores within Metro Atlanta," or your business can get much deeper by stating, "We will generate $1 million in revenue from the ten new stores we plan to open in Metro Atlanta." This is now an easy blueprint to follow throughout the year because you can now track your progress based on where you are financially toward that goal.

It is also extremely motivating for employees to be able to see that their work is adding to the success of the company and its goals. Imagine attending a sporting event where each team is playing as hard as they can but no one is keeping score. How motivated would the players be to continue playing? How motivated would you be to continue watching them play with no score being recorded? Take score in your business, and do not be afraid of the numbers; instead, embrace them.

ATTAINABLE

It is also important not to go overboard in goal setting. The quickest way to take away the motivation of great people is to make them feel that they can never achieve the goal no matter how hard they try. Remember, the top brands we talked about in the opening of this book were not built overnight, so remember things take time to develop. Also know that lots of business plans are discarded by banks every year because of unrealistic goals and unachievable growth estimates that make businesses appear that they didn't do the proper research. Be sure to research the industry your business is in to have a proper understanding of the growth potential.

REALISTIC

Simply put, understand what can be realistically achieved by your business given all available resources. You may have an ice cream truck that wants to sell one million ice cream cones, but is that realistic to do in the middle of winter in Chicago? Probably not. Be honest with your team about the realities of the business prior to moving forward, so everyone understands the challenges ahead. This helps you and your team avoid feeling discouraged.

TIME-BASED

This is the most critical objective that every business must follow in order to be successful. There must be a defined timeline in the goal setting process which states when the results will be achieved. If you miss the deadline for achieving the goal, it's okay. As long as you followed all the above steps, you should not be that far away from what you originally planned.

It's recommended that you employ the SMART strategy with every goal your business attempts in order to ensure you are always following a well-defined template for success. (The SMART Goals Worksheet below can help with this.) After setting the SMART goal, you then want to break out specific tasks and activities that will help you accomplish each goal. Do not be afraid to make adjustments along the way, because successful businesses remain nimble and ready to pivot in another direction if a major roadblock develops.

By utilizing the SWOT analysis and SMART strategy on all your business goals along the way, your business will already be steps ahead of the competition. Please do not overlook these valuable tools in your brand-building process.

CHART 1.3. SMART GOALS WORKSHEET

	Answers at the time of development	Quarterly update
Specific: ⬜ What is the desired result? (who, what, where, when, and how)		
Measurable: ⬜ What is the trackable result which you can count numerically? (time, money, statistics, etc.)		
Achievable: ⬜ What is necessary for the business to succeed? ⬜ How will the business environment impact your goals? ⬜ What things need to be accomplished?		
Relevant: ⬜ Is the goal in alignment with the overall strategy?		
Time-Based: ⬜ What is the time-line for success? ⬜ What are the set deadlines to reach the goals?		

Now that we have discussed the SMART strategy for setting goals (specific, measurable, attainable, realistic, and time- based). You will use that strategy and take some time to write down your business goals in order to prepare for the bright future that is coming to you. The final part of this chapter involves completing a short- and long-term goal assessment in order to provide you with what is going to be needed in your business plan. Assessing your goals will also help you envision all that will be required to be successful with your business, which should excite you. Take some time to answer these final questions so we can begin the next phase of building your brand.

1. What are the short-term goals of the business (months 1-12)?
2. What are the long-term goals of the business (months 12-36)?

When listing the short- and long-term goals, I am sure that you will list a lot of great ideas about your personal passions for the future of your business, but also include financial projections for the income statement, which you will have to prepare in the business plan later. Here are a few categories to consider:

1. Price of product or service
2. Product sales goals
3. Sales revenue estimates
4. Expected operating expenses (office space, utilities, employees, etc.)
5. Income statement: Revenue (c) – Expenses (d) = Net Income

Making money from your business should always be the goal, but without realistic financial data, your business will have a weak foundation, which is one of the main reasons so many companies fail within the first twelve months. Potential investors will also want to see your financial projections, so it's always good to have an idea of what your financial outlook is well in advance. The companies that become successful are the companies that have professional financial projections and well- defined goals for the future with measurable targets.

Once you have completed everything in this step, you are ready to start step 2, building your business website.

STEP 1: ACTION CHECKLIST

- [ ] Create a legal business entity
  - [ ] C CORPORATION
  - [ ] S CORPORATION
  - [ ] LIMITED LIABILITY COMPANY (LLC)
  - [ ] PARTNERSHIP
  - [ ] SOLE PROPRIETORSHIP
- [ ] DETERMINING A NAME FOR YOUR BUSINESS
- [ ] REGISTER YOUR CORPORATION WITH IRS
- [ ] CONSULT WITH AN ATTORNEY
- [ ] CONSULT WITH A CERTIFIED PUBLIC ACCOUNTANT
- [ ] RESEARCH PAYROLL COMPANIES
- [ ] SHORT- AND LONG-TERM GOAL ASSESSMENT
- [ ] SWOT ANALYSIS
- [ ] SMART STRATEGY

STEP 2: BUILD

This chapter will discuss the key elements needed to build a professional- quality business website that will give your business the ability to be found on the Internet by people that may want to spend money with your company. It does not matter whether you are creating your website yourself or hiring someone else to do it for you, because the process is the same.

There are essential elements that every business website must contain regardless of the type of business you have, so as you read through this chapter, please apply the concepts to your specific business or industry. When choosing your website name, make sure you do your research by looking at competitors within your industry that have similar business models that are both successful and unsuccessful. By doing this, you can learn from the positives and negatives of others in your industry in order to properly position your business for success.

Now that you have taken a look at your competitors' websites URLs, it is time to determine your own. You may be tempted, but do not pick any website names too close to your competitors' name. Although you may be trying to steal business from them, it may have the opposite effect of irritating potential customers searching for that specific business.

There is no need to rush this process, because your website URL name is one of the most important pieces of branding your company to potential clients, because it is your business identity on the Internet. Try to pick a name that is easy to remember as well as one that applies directly to your industry. There are some general best practices when it comes to choosing your domain name, which are listed here in their order of importance:

CHOOSING THE RIGHT DOMAIN NAME

Your website name should stand out by being easy to remember instantly by anyone that sees or hears it. Understand that using slang words (OK instead of okay) or even words that can be spelled or pronounced multiple ways (phat vs. fat) can lead to instant confusion when someone is searching for your website. As your marketing budget grows, you can afford to influence the public to go to any site you want them to, but if you currently lack a million-dollar national advertising budget, then it's best to keep it simple. If consumers can't find your website during an initial search, most don't give you the benefit of the doubt as a small business; instead, they assume you did something incorrectly in relaying your URL to them or spelled something wrong. Keep your domain name short if possible because otherwise you take a chance on a consumer mistyping or incorrectly spelling the web address, and if this occurs, most people will never try to visit your website again.

Use keywords that are relevant to your product or industry within your domain name. This way your business URL will appear higher in an organic search on the Internet. Examples of how to properly use keywords for a cosmetic dentist that specializes in dental implants, for instance, would be to use words in their website URL such as "cosmetic dentist" or "dental implants." Think of words that your friends or family may use when searching for your type of product of service, and then think of a creative way to incorporate those words into your website URL. Doing the above- mentioned things will help your website appear higher organically when someone is doing a general search in their website browser. This, in turn, will increase your site traffic.

USE GEOGRAPHIC LOCATION IN YOUR URL

When selecting your URL, also think of adding a reference to where you are located, especially if you are a neighborhood store or if you primarily service a particular area. Consider using the name of your city, state, or neighborhood that you primarily service in your URL. This is a great way to identify yourself as a local business to consumers within those areas and make the name of your business easier to remember. An example would be www.MainStreetBarbershop.org or www.ForestParkDental.org; these URLs let potential clients know exactly what area the businesses serve as well as what their service is.

BUY URL MISSPELLINGS OF YOUR NAME

To some this may sound like a crazy concept as well as a big waste of money. Go tell that to all the major brands of the world that do this all the time. Think about it; if you are JeffsAuto.org, how much would it diminish your business if your local competitor bought JeffAuto.org, JeffsAutos.org, and JeffAutos.org? How many of your potential clients do you think would make those common typing mistakes every day when searching for your business? You would hate for this to happen to your business after you have worked hard to build a name for yourself, but unfortunately, this happens every day to small businesses just like ours.

STAY CLEAR OF COMMON MISTAKES

Do not use numbers, hyphens, or special characters in your URL because people sometime misunderstand them.

Consumers also may not know if you mean the number (1) or the word (one), so it's best to avoid using them in your website name. Once again, if the consumers make that mistake, it is still your fault as a business for not ensuring your URL is clearly understood by all. You also want to create website URLs that stand out. This is extremely important because you want to make sure your URL name gets noticed amongst the millions of other registered domains of similar products, services, or ideas out there.

DO YOUR RESEARCH

Far too many small business owners enter the market without fully understanding the who, what, why, and where of their local and national competitors. It is important to know these things because you don't want to get sued by other corporations for violating trademarks and copyrights. Lawsuits interfere with you doing business and cost you money regardless of the outcome, so make sure you do your due diligence in researching the URL name you chose.

HOW TO BUY YOUR DOMAIN NAME (URL)

Congratulations! You have chosen your domain name. Now there are some very simple steps you need to take to purchase that domain name and register it, so that once your website is built, it will appear on the World Wide Web.

STEP 1: CHOOSE A DOMAIN REGISTRAR

There are a variety of companies to choose from when trying to register your domain, do a search on the Internet for the least expensive domain registrars, because registering your domain should not cost you that much. Also, ask around to other business owners to see who they utilize. Avoid signing up immediately for the first one you find, because choosing the wrong registrar can cost you up to ten times of what you should pay for one. Your domain name should not cost you more than $14 per year, so please do yourself a favor and search for the more well-known companies on the Internet and try to avoid domain resellers that will charge you high monthly fees that are more than the annual cost of the domain name registration with a non-reseller.

STEP 2: CHOOSE ANONYMOUS REGISTRATION

To avoid being contacted by every salesperson in the world, choose the anonymous URL registration. This will limit the personal information disclosed about you. On Whois.com anyone can view details like your name, phone number, company name, and address of the person that registered the website. All of this information becomes publicly available by default, but you have the option of hiding it from public view. This may be free to do or come with an added cost depending on who you choose to register your site with. Doing this will save you countless hours of answering calls from telemarketers, as well as provide anonymity to the business owner that registered the website.

STEP 3: WEBSITE HOSTING

Now that you have officially registered your domain name, you still do not have a website, just an address where that newly built website can accept traffic once completed. What you need to do at this stage is decide who will build and host your website, which also comes with additional cost. Think of it as buying a lot of land; now you have to go out and find someone to build you a new home or build it yourself. Regardless of which option you choose, there is also a hosting fee associated with housing your website and its data so it will be available on demand whenever someone searches for your URL online.

KEY ELEMENTS REQUIRED FOR A PROFESSIONAL WEBSITE

By definition, a website is the virtual business card for your brand. Without it you run the risk of looking unprofessional to any potential clients you may be working hard to impress. However, you can't just have any old website. There are also certain elements every professional website must have to ensure your business goals are achieved. Not including any of these necessary elements within the pages of your website will lead to a less robust and user-friendly website, not to mention all the money you will be wasting with your future marketing efforts guiding consumers to an ineffective website.

CALL TO ACTION

When someone comes to your website, you must give them something to do immediately or they will leave the website, especially if it is a new-brand company and the consumer is unfamiliar with your products or services. Calls-to-action are buttons or links, preferably within the top portion of your website, that tell consumers what to do next if they choose to do business with you. When creating this call to action, it is important that you first think hard about what you want the outcome to be for any consumer that comes to your website. The possible actions you want a consumer to take once they are on your site determine how your site should be designed in order to achieve the goal or purpose of your website. There are five potential actions a consumer may take when visiting a business website, which are as follows:

1. Purchase something on the website
2. Make a phone call to the business
3. Fill out a form (sign up for a newsletter or email list, contact us or make an inquiry)
4. Visit the location of the business based on the location(s) listed on the website
5. Research products or services

It is important that your call to action uses the proper language to engage the consumer and make them want to take the desired action. Keep in mind, having a form pop up immediately when someone comes to your website may not be the best idea, because you run the risk of turning the consumer off if they are not familiar with your brand. Instead, that same form can be embedded within your call-to-action link. That way the consumer feels they are making the choice to complete the forms or newsletters versus being forced to do so in order to proceed.

AN IMPRESSIVE HOME PAGE

The website home page is the first thing consumers will see when they click on your URL, so it is important that you clearly communicate the purpose and image of your brand to the consumer. It can be tempting to go overboard on your home page by adding flash media and animation into the design to try to impress website visitors. Unfortunately, these types of images can increase load time and in some cases not even appear depending on the user's device. This is why you must learn to impress consumers with a clean professional site that has purpose versus lots of bells and whistles that do nothing to improve the consumer's website experience. Keep it simple! Let your products or services impress the consumer, not the design (unless you are selling design services). A good website should immediately inform the visitor of the following things about your brand:

1. Who your business serves (those searching for a personal injury attorney, women's apparel, children's toys, etc.)
2. What your business has to offer (products, services, sales, and specials)
3. Where you do business (geographic area or locations you serve)
4. When you are open for business (hours of operation, seasonality)
5. Why the consumer should do business with you (what sets you apart from other brands that do the same thing)
6. How the consumer can initiate a business transaction with your brand (call to action button, phone call, email, etc.)

BY CHRISTOPH DYER

BUSINESS LOGO

Your home page must also include your business logo, which is a symbol, wording, or design that you choose to represent your business. The chosen logo will be used to gain instant brand recognition in all future marketing materials, apparel, vehicles, etc.; therefore it should represent the values of your brand as well as appeal to your target consumer group. Limit the number of colors in your logo so it can be easily duplicated in all formats without changing the original design, which can confuse the consumer.

When designing your logo, make sure it is something that will still look nice visually and is legible even if it's the size of your thumbnail. Taking the thumbnail approach to building your logo will assist you in not going overboard on the design by forcing you to keep it simple. This has always been a touchy subject to some business owners, mainly because brands are extremely prideful of their logo. So when someone tells them that it looks bad and needs to be changed in order to be legible in an advertisement, some brands get angry. However, if they choose not to heed the advice, the consumer is left confused about the brand, which only hurts your business.

Think about this scenario: Your brand has been chosen to sponsor a major event in your area, and your logo will be printed on all the marketing materials for the event. There is one problem, though: your logo is a picture of a purple panda with the words "Purple Panda Healthy Juice Bar" going around the panda in white lettering, but the marketing materials for the event have a white background, and the printer printed the panda in red by mistake.

Unfortunately, as a sponsor, you have no control over any of the printing of the marketing materials, so now your logo appears as a red panda without the wording being visible due to the white background. Sounds crazy, but unfortunately it happens all the time, which leaves the brand in the predicament of not being properly represented. The event organizer will simply tell you, "Sorry but your logo did not meet the standards needed to appear properly in all the marketing materials, but we did our job by including it." You will not be receiving a refund of the sponsorship fees you invested. You will just learn a lesson and have a lot of confused consumers wondering what the red panda on the flier represents.

USER-FRIENDLY NAVIGATION

Visitors to your website must be able to easily find the information they are searching for, so it is important that the menu bar is easy to find. According to kissmetrics.com, bad navigation is the number one reason people will abandon your website. This means that you must properly structure your menu bar into categories that the user can understand so they can easily navigate to find information on your website. A major issue that sometimes interferes with user navigation is that with mobile websites, the menu bar usually appears as three lines in one of the upper corners of the page. For this reason, you may want to think about having the core information contained within your home page so the user is not confused about how to find the menu bar.

Think hard about how to structure your menu bar by first understanding what questions about your brand consumers need answered immediately when they come to your website. The questions include the following: What broad categories of products or services do you offer? What do they cost? What location or areas do you service? What are your hours of operation? How do they purchase these products or services? What forms of payment do you accept?

You want to clearly identify the areas of your website the consumer needs to visit in order to gather all the information they need to do business with your brand. Limiting the number of times visitors to your website have to click on things to uncover information about your products or services will increase the likelihood that they will do business with you, as well as increase the overall user experience. The goal should be to keep the menu bar simple and clean so your potential consumers will be able to find information quickly.

SEARCH FEATURE

Another great thing to include in your new website is a search box feature, which allows visitors to type in words or phrases to find what they are looking for instantly. This does not replace the menu bar, but instead offers website visitors more options to get them to the information they are seeking. The search box works really well for a business that has tons of inventory or services to choose from, by allowing the consumer to be presented with relevant pages related only to the keywords they type in. This is great for millennials that want information immediately and don't have the time nor the patience to search page by page for that one item they really want to purchase. Including the search box feature will increase the overall user experience, providing the consumer with the ability to navigate your website the way they want to without limitations.

MOBILE FRIENDLY

In these busy times we live in, most of us rely heavily on our mobile devices for everything from engaging with an app to reading the latest news clip. We love viewing things on the go. According to a Pew Research Center 2017 study, 77 percent of Americans own smartphones compared to only 73 percent of people that have Internet at home. This means your website must include responsive design to make sure users can view it on any type of device, especially smart phones and mobile devices. It is best to not make website users have to pinch or expand the screen to view the website data, because this can lead to problems with navigating the website and/or finding the information the user is visiting the website for. You want to have a responsive website that automatically adjusts the website dimensions based on the screen size of the device the user is using. Choose a responsive site over the option of having a web and mobile version of your website, mainly because the search engines tend to view these as two different websites, which can lead to your website not appearing as high in the organic search results online.

QUALITY CONTENT

Making strong and bold statements about your business is a key element to building a professional website. Being able to properly project confidence about your business as well as being informative about your products or services can lead to a great user experience, which will increase the time on your website and reduce the bounce rate. Bounce rate is defined as the percentage of people who land on a page on your website and then leave without clicking on anything else or navigating to any other pages on your site.

Average time on page is just as it sounds: it is simply the average amount of time all visitors spend on a particular page. Developing quality content can aide you in increasing these two key analytics by providing the user with engaging material which they are seeking, in the clearest way possible. It is also very important not to go overboard with non-relevant content on your website, because the user will get bored quickly with useless material.

QUALITY DESIGN

Your website design is crucial to projecting the proper image about your business to everyone that visits. Make sure your website stands out with a clear, well thought-out layout that is comparable to that of other companies in your industry. This means that if you are a wellness spa, emphasizing the clean, calming environment within the spa with elegant photos on the home page will help you attract new clients. If you have a clothing store, it would be good to showcase your inventory immediately when someone arrives on the home page. Limiting the number of clicks it takes for a user to find what they are looking for will increase the power of your brand overall. Look at the websites of some of the major companies in your industry. You will notice that the brands that do it right try to put their product or service in front of you immediately when you arrive on the website. The amateurs tend to place a lot of barriers in between the visitor and the product or service information. Those amateurs may do things like put newsletter popups on the homepage or have the company bio take up the entire top half of the home page. This will not be what you will do after reading this book.

Always update your content regularly to keep it

relevant and current, because frequent visitors to your website are paying attention to how recent your content is. Relevant content is really important for any inventory-based business, so it's important to keep your product or service menu updated regularly. For example, have you ever seen a product or service listed on a brand's website, but when you went to the store it was discontinued or no longer in stock? Do not run your business this way. Instead, show customers that you are a professional brand that can be trusted to do business with. It is also a great idea to have a blog attached to your website so you can discuss topics relevant to your industry. This also gives clients the perception that you are a responsive business.

If you are a person that does not have the time to make regular updates to a blog, there is a great option that exists called an RSS feed. RSS means rich site summary, but it is also often referred to as really simple syndication because it is a type of web news feed which allows users to access content relevant to their industry or business that is constantly updated by the source of the feed. Having an RSS feed on your website allows new content to come to your website in one centralized location.

You simply add the RSS feed reader to your website during the design process and then research the best RSS feed based on your type of brand. For example, if you are a marketing agency website, there are some great RSS feeds from various advertising blog sites that update with new content four times a day. In the eyes of your clients, it will appear that you are constantly staying abreast of the information relevant to marketing, while behind the scenes you are allowing yourself more time to grow your company. So whether you use impressive images, video, or lively animation, the most important thing is creating an interactive user experience that differentiates your website from the competitions'.

REVIEWS

Tell everyone that visits your brand's website what others think about you. According to Bright Local, "88 percent of consumers trust online reviews as much as a personal recommendation—which is astounding, considering most online reviews are posted by total strangers. The same survey found that only 12 percent of the population did not regularly read reviews for consumer products." What this study demonstrates is that consumers increasingly want to know who they are doing business with; the veil of secrecy needs to be lifted in order to be effective as a brand in this age. Adding your social media icons to your homepage will also allow for more transparency by allowing users to make comments about you that you can then respond to in real time, making for a truly valuable consumer experience. Do not fall victim to the urge to send angry responses to negative comments on review and social sites. As you have probably seen online in various contexts, this only makes you look childish and will lead to a negative impact on your brand eventually. You should also have share buttons throughout your website which will allow visitors to share information about your products or services with others, which will in turn lead to more interest and awareness in your brand.

STEP 2: BUILD CHECKLIST

- ☐ CHOOSING THE RIGHT DOMAIN NAME
- ☐ USE GEOGRAPHIC LOCATION IN YOUR URL
- ☐ BUY URL MISSPELLINGS OF YOUR NAME
- ☐ STAY CLEAR OF COMMON MISTAKES
- ☐ DO YOUR RESEARCH
- ☐ HOW TO BUY YOUR DOMAIN NAME (URL)
    - ☐ STEP 1: CHOOSE A DOMAIN REGISTRAR
    - ☐ STEP 2: CHOOSE ANONYMOUS REGISTRATION
    - ☐ STEP 3: WEBSITE HOSTING
- ☐ KEY ELEMENTS REQUIRED FOR A PROFESSIONAL WEBSITE
    - ☐ CALL TO ACTION
    - ☐ AN IMPRESSIVE HOME PAGE
    - ☐ BUSINESS LOGO
    - ☐ USER-FRIENDLY NAVIGATION
    - ☐ SEARCH FEATURE
    - ☐ MOBILE FRIENDLY
    - ☐ QUALITY CONTENT
    - ☐ QUALITY DESIGN
    - ☐ REVIEWS

BY CHRISTOPH DYER

STEP 3: CREATE

Now that you have successfully turned your idea into a legal business entity and built a professional website, it is time to begin setting up your presence on social media. There are some important steps to follow in creating your social media profiles to ensure you are projecting professionalism as well as developing engaging content that will get shared and talked about by the right people. In this chapter we will discuss what those elements are to get your business booming on social media. Please do not underestimate the power of social media and think it's only for teens chattering about nothing. Social media is one of the most powerful ways to engage consumers as well as promote your business in a neutral environment that's non-invasive to the consumer. Being effective on social media starts with having a plan for each social media channel that you feel best fits your strategy. In developing the strategy, first determine which social media platforms your target audience is utilizing. This can be done in a variety of ways.

Start by asking some questions about the social media sites being used by your chosen consumer group. Determine how they socialize amongst their peers using social media. Do they mostly share photos, videos, or text only? This is important because it will let you know which sites are going to be your main priority for posting about your business initially, because unless you have a lot of time or a staff in place to post for you, being on too many social media sites can be overwhelming. Luckily, there are several options of social media management tools available through various websites that allow you to schedule your posts months in advance and pick multiple social media sites to deliver your messages to.

These management tools are a great way to stay on top of your content posting schedule. They also save you from having to pay someone else to post for you, which can cost up to $50 each post with some companies. Social media posting is something you should control yourself as a business, because no one else knows your company and its products the way you do. Most digital marketing companies that you pay to post for you will mainly post general content that won't talk directly about your daily operations and what you are doing in the community you serve, which is what social users want to see.

Today, social media users want to feel that they can trust your company in order to confidently do business with you and refer their friends to shop with you. The more they know about your brand and feel they really know your business, the more likely they are to spend money with you. Also, the more you know about the people that will become customers the better you can tune your brand identity to them over time. Knowing why people like your products or services helps you deliver posts that talk directly about what your customer actually cares about. Put a plan in writing so you and your team can refer back to it later whenever you need to verify if your posts are meeting your goals for your brand. Your social media strategy should be sectioned out for each social media channel that you plan to use for expanding your business. If you do not have employees to assist with your social media content posting, then it may be a good idea to start with no more than three social media channels, even if you are using a social media management tool.

Social media does more than just allow you to make friends with your potential clients or customers. It also allows you to market directly to people that are within your chosen geographic area that have expressed interest in whatever celebrity, brand, product, or service you choose when you initially set up the social media marketing campaign. We will discuss how to market on social media later. For now we will discuss some best practices of professionalism when using social media for your brand. By the end of this chapter your business venture will be one step closer to becoming the brand you have always envisioned it to be. But as the old saying goes, "You can lead a horse to water but you can't make him drink," so be sure to apply this formula to building your brand on social media. Your business's success is up to you!

As Henry Ford said, "Whether you think you can or whether you think you can't, you're right."

SOCIAL MEDIA PAGE LAYOUT

The way you design a page for social media is a bit different from how you design a website, but there are some similarities. The things that should remain consistent across your website and social pages are your company's branding, advertising, and call to action. The images on your social media pages fall into three categories: profile picture, cover/banner image, and you may have a background as well. Your company logo should always be displayed as the profile picture. Hopefully you followed the steps we discussed in chapter 2 about designing the proper logo; if you did that, then your logo will look great in the profile picture spot. Next, the cover/banner and background images should showcase your products or services as well as include a call to action of some kind. Every brand should always have some type of promotion or campaign going on in order to constantly engage your potential consumers.

Using the proper image sizes and high resolution for social media profiles is extremely important in order to project the professionalism of your brand. Before uploading the images to your social media site, make sure they comply with the file size recommendations of the platform. Chart 3.1 below lists the size recommendations for the various social media platforms' cover, profile, and background images.

CHART 3.1. SOCIAL MEDIA IMAGE SIZES

Facebook Image Size	Instagram Image Size
Profile image: 180 x 180 Cover photo: 820 x 310 Shared images: 1200 x 630 Shared link: 1200 x 627 Event image: 1920 x 1080	Profile image: 110 x 110 Photo thumbnails: 161 x 161 Photo size: 1080 x 1080 Video to stories: 750 x 1334 Portrait: 1080 x 1350 pixels
Twitter Image Size	Google Plus Image Size
Header photo: 1500 x 500 Profile photo: 400 x 400 Instream photo: 440 x 220	Profile image: 250 x 250 Cover photo: 1080 x 608 Shared images: 497 x 373 Shared video: 497 x 279 Shared image in feed: 150 x 150

Also ensure that your social media design is visually consistent across all platforms. By keeping the same design, look, and feel across all platforms, you are building your brand identity for potential consumers. Now when they see a similar design somewhere else throughout your brand-building efforts, they will instantly associate it with your product or service.

Visual consistency is one of the most important things in the overall brand-building process because a consumer has to be exposed to your brand about 3.2 times on average before they commit it to memory. Therefore, you have to have a cohesive identity for all of your brand marketing efforts so you give the consumer as many opportunities as possible to be exposed to your brand. Constantly changing your social images is not a problem. Just make sure that what you do for one page you do for all pages, so your clients are not left confused about the goal of your brand.

Keep in mind that images matter more than text on social media just due to the nature of how most consumers utilize social media platforms. We have become a scroll and swipe society in which we try to consume information quickly. If what is being viewed is not visually appealing, the consumer will just swipe or scroll past in less than a millisecond. Our brains actually consume images a thousand times faster than they process words and text.

Images have been known to generate more engagement and sharing versus text, especially when those images include people. Keep your text limited to less than 20 percent within any images on social media, which used to be the Facebook rule for cover photos, so just try to stick to it and keep mainly image-based content.

It is a great idea to research the guidelines of each social media venue to ensure you are not violating any of their rules. You should look over the social media guidelines prior to investing any capital into designing content, to save yourself from wasting one dime. The majority of these guidelines forbid nudity, obscene or threatening images/content, profanity, and copyrighted images not owned by your business. This includes any type of music or voice composition as well, so please save yourself the headache of trying to make your favorite song run in a social ad campaign, because it will get rejected nine out of ten times. Understanding the social media guidelines can be critical to your business. If you choose to ignore or violate any of them, your page can be terminated and permanently blocked from using the platform. So take the time to review each social media platform's posting and content guidelines, which are ever changing in this digital world.

The number one rule that you should always follow at the end of the day is to keep it simple, especially when it comes to marketing your brand on social media. As discussed previously, we live in a scroll and swipe society. Therefore users need to be instantly engaged by your content, or else they move on. For any promotional campaign for your brand utilizing social media, you must use compelling images, make simple statements in your wording, and have a distinct call to action. This means that the design contained within your banner/cover images must be compelling and effectively indicate what your call to action is in the simplest way possible. For example, if you have a new product coming to the market, your call to action should clearly address the main questions the consumer needs answered about your product/service, such as the features and benefits of doing business with you instead of the competitor. Clearly identify your advantage in the market to the consumer up front on your cover image. Whether you have a lower price than everyone else or a superior offering, you must spell it out to even get the consumer intrigued by your new brand.

The final but most important suggestion about creating your social media profiles is to be as creative as possible and make things visually engaging to your audience. Having a proper understanding of who your audience is plays a major role in creating the best content that will get your followers buzzing. The bottom line is this: The only reason to even use social media is to engage with your audience and get them sharing content about your brand, in an effort to grow revenue. That's all that matters. For this reason, your content needs to appeal visually to the people you want to spend money on your brand. When it does, they are more likely to share it with friends to increase your social media page traffic. Feel free to be as creative as possible, without being over the top or offensive with your visuals and while limiting your text as much as possible. If done effectively, adhering to these simple guidelines for developing your social media pages will help increase your overall visibility in the marketplace in which you want to do business.

CONTENT POSTING

Create a chart that provides details of how you plan to segment your social media posts in order to accomplish your brand's goals. Here are a few different approaches your business can use to segment your social media posts. Please feel free to use any or all of them to assist you in your social media branding efforts.

THE TOP-DOWN APPROACH

50 percent of the content you post will drive your audience back to your website, such as original stories and blog posts you created.

25 percent of the content you post will come from other sources, such as news articles, inspirational stories, and quotes from celebrities and industry thought leaders.

20 percent of the content you post supports your business objectives, such as sales, product promotions, events, and other revenue-generating things.

5 percent of the content you post will be about the community you serve and positive stories that impact them.

The 80-20 Approach

80 percent of the content you post should be for the purpose of informing, educating, inspiring or entertaining your social media audience.

20 percent of the remaining content you post is dedicated to promoting your products, services, or events in an effort to generate sales.

The Rule of Thirds Approach

One-third of your content posts should promote your brand, advertise products and services, and generate revenue.

One-third of your content posts should be shared information from experts in the industry, quotes, or stories from like-minded business leaders that inspire.

One-third of your content posts should enable an open dialogue between your business and your audience. This could begin with posting questions, thoughts, and ideas that invite the audience to comment in a positive way.

DEVELOP A SOCIAL MEDIA POSTING CALENDAR

Creating an advertising calendar for all of your social media channels will allow you to operate your business the right way by putting time into each post to ensure it aligns with your overall mission and company image. The calendar should clearly define dates, times, and content that you want to be delivered on the various social media sites. Take your time with this calendar because it will become the backbone of your branding strategy moving forward. When creating it, think long and hard about the image you want to project to the public about your business. Carefully craft the wording within each post to ensure you are speaking directly to your audience based on the research you previously did. Also, limit the text within any advertising campaign because today's consumers want to quickly consume information. If you were planning to post an ad with a biography on your business within it or a long explanation of why people should do business with you, please refrain from doing this. It will only hurt you. The consumer will not invest large amounts of time reading lots of words in your ad, so instead try to find creative ways to explain things simplistically. Begin to compile the images, links, and videos that you will use for each post, because organization is the key to being successful in business.

    Consistency is crucial for any growing brand, so you want to appear to have things in order at every step of this process. If you forget to post for weeks or months, it can be detrimental to everything you have built because to the consumer, you appear not to be an active, relevant, or dependable brand that can handle their needs.

    Now that you understand how to organize and schedule posts so you consistently stay in front of your audience, let's discuss some tips for making your social media posts effective so they impact the people you want to reach.

CREDIBILITY POST

Building credibility for your brand involves posting things that do not ask your social media users to take any action, and instead aim to establish your brand as service or product ambassadors within your industry. Credibility posts may not get shared as much, but they help to show your audience that you care about the community as well as other people in the world. Sharing press releases, news about your company, community service events that you took part in and articles about things that your audience may be passionate about can lead to increased interaction on your social media pages. If you are a personal trainer, for example, you could post an article about an Olympic athlete's workout routine in an effort to show your clients the possibilities that exist if they follow your workout plan. A vegan chef could post that same article but write a comment about the healthy eating side of the Olympic athlete's routine with a comment such as, "Six packs are made in the kitchen." The options are endless when it comes to commenting on news and current events, as long as it directly relates to your business goals.

You do not want to risk leaving your audience confused about the direction of your brand by posting things just because they seem interesting. The goal of a post on social media should be to successfully connect the dots between a current event that your audience may be interested in and your brand's image to drive home a natural connection between the two. Your audience needs to see a direct correlation between your brand and the news or events you are posting about. You must do a good job in your comments to further connect the dots so the reader understands what the article has to do with your brand, especially if your company is not directly being mentioned in the article. It is very important that you verify the authenticity of any news articles that are posted to your social media pages so you do not ruin your credibility by posting fake news articles and attempting to connect them to your business. This can make you appear not to be a credible business in the eyes of your social media followers, so just take the extra step of making sure the article is accurate before you post it to your business page.

Take a look at what's going on in the world as well as within your industry to find these interesting articles that will make excellent posts. Think about popular events that are coming up or currently going on that your audience has an interest in. A great tip for any event planner is to always post events, whether you are involved with those events or not, because it gets your audience used to you being the hub of event information in the area. So when the time comes for your next event, your audience is already salivating waiting to hear about it because they are used to you only posting about the premiere events. This is in no way meant to deceive your audience into thinking that you are involved with all of the events you're posting about, but perception does sometimes become reality in your audience's mind, and it doesn't hurt if they think you are an active brand. Credibility posts assist you in building your brand's awareness within the market, which over time will pay off for your growing business by keeping your brand on the minds of consumers. People want to know that you are a real person when communicating about your business on social media, so it is important to not always focus on selling them something. Instead use creditability posts to show the human side of your business by posting about major things that are affecting real people around the world. Post about the sports team that won the national championship, or the new exhibit coming to town, or post of your condolences for well-known people that have passed away. All these types of posts help in boosting your creditability on social media, which will go far beyond the coupons you post daily.

POST REGULARLY AND BUILD RELATIONSHIPS

A great content posting strategy involves posting at least three times per day on each social media channel in order to dominate the timeline or newsfeed of the social media users. Social media timelines move extremely fast because of the number of people users are following, so without routine posting you may not even appear on someone's timeline at all during the day. The consumer group you have chosen is likely to have hundreds if not thousands of other people and brands that they are following, so it's easy for them to forget you. Therefore, posting once a day just will not cut it in today's fast-moving society, because of the demands that come with content posting as discussed earlier.

The posting plan you create is crucial in order to keep up with your audience, so you are never forgotten by anyone and are able to build a solid brand that people know is relevant to their daily lives. In the next step in this book, we will discuss how to develop a posting matrix in order to plan your posting strategy to align with your brand image you are building. It is rare for things to happen by accident in the business world, so plan for everything, even if it seems trivial. You are building something you want your staff to be able to duplicate, so write your strategy down and follow it.

Posting about things that will allow your social media

followers to interact with you, instead of just pushing your products on them, is an excellent way to build the relationships you need to sustain your brand over time. Showing humor through funny, non-offensive content within your posts is the perfect way to do this. Also, creating visually stunning infographics with interesting quotes or facts seems to go a long way nowadays on social media and generates tons of likes, shares, and re-tweets. Engage the community you want your brand to represent by not being afraid to say things that will get people talking about your brand—without offending anyone, of course.

The goal of relationship-building posts should be to cement the relationship between your brand and the consumers in your market. Building relationships means you like other users' posts, comment on what they share, and make them feel that you noticed them. Be an active part of the social media lives of your followers in order to further your business name in the marketplace, which will have lasting effects on your brand.

Interact with your audience, which is one of the most overlooked things by so many brands using social media today. Sharing links is good, but you can't just do that nonstop without actually engaging with your audience and replying to comments. Because this is so important, some social media networks actually display how responsive your brand is, mainly to emails and phone calls, through their platform. Just take this a step further by being responsive to the comments that users place on your post every day.

The true social media engagement happens through interacting on the various social networks, because this lets your audience know that you are an active brand in the market that they can get a response from you in the future if something goes wrong with whatever they buy from you. Your followers also want a quality response that reflects who you are as a brand, so make sure you are not replying to comments at 3:00 a.m. after a night of partying. You want to avoid a chance of saying something the wrong way or making clerical errors that will make your audience question your creditability overall.

MAKE PEOPLE WANT TO FOLLOW YOU

In today's busy world full of information coming at us 24/7, it can be hard for any brand to stand out amongst all the clutter. Social media platforms provide users with thousands of choices of where to gather information on everything from news, to events, to the latest product releases. Therefore, when posting, you have to think from the users' perspective so you are able to stand out in the crowd.

Think to yourself who would have an interest in following your business and why. It is extremely important to your brand that you are able to grab your followers' attention by having the best industry-leading content contained within your social media pages. Are you offering discounts, coupons, and behind-the-scenes content and helping followers solve a problem? What is your thing that sets you apart on social media? You have to figure this out early on so you can always stay ahead of your competitors. If someone can see the same content on your page in twenty other places, then your brand has no value to them. I'm sure we have all seen brands that seem great and then go out of business, not because they didn't have a good product, but because they lacked any type of competitive advantage to make the consumer choose to shop with them over the competitor. This is how you must view every single post you place on social media, because it only takes one time to make a bad impression.

Along with this, like we touched on earlier, only publish content on your social media pages that is consistent with your brand identity and builds value for your brand. This content should be simultaneously helpful, relevant, and entertaining to your audience. This can be hard, but it is required to have an effective post every time. Quality is far superior to quantity. Therefore, don't rush the posting process by not being structured in what you are delivering to your audience. The last thing you want is for your number of followers to decline because you post irrelevant or offensive content that does not resonate well with your audience. Also do not over post about your business throughout the day to users that may not want to constantly be bombarded with your content. Post things that are general market that most people will like and not be offended by, such as cats, dogs, and babies, which seem to make everyone smile. Some people may say it is good to shock people with out-of-the-ordinary things, but by doing that you run the risk of being blocked, unfriended, and reported, which are not good things for a business on the rise.

TARGETING YOUR AUDIENCE

The people that choose to follow your brand are not all the same. They come from diverse backgrounds, and each of them identify with your brand for various reasons. Never overlook anyone when promoting on social media, because you never know who is actually reading what you are posting.

Video game users may primarily be teenagers, but the major video game buyers are largely adults, parents buying games for their kids. So your social media posts should target each of your potential consumers in an effort to appeal to the various audience segments that may exist for your brand. Major soda brands are experts at having a variety of posts that target each demographic separately, such as one post to target millennials, which speaks about the fun and the excitement of being young; and another post reminding brand loyalists that the product hasn't changed in years with statements like, "The same taste you remember," or some version of that.

Invite your audience into the conversation by creating a two-way conversation with them by asking engaging questions. Any post that invites conversation will help in this process, so ask for opinions on new products or services from your audience in order to get people engaging with your brand. Posts that ask your audience yes or no questions are a great engagement tactic that will help you gather opinions so you can gauge whether to bring a new product to market or not. You can also share blog content from popular sites that your audience likes in an effort to create more post engagement. It can be a struggle to constantly develop new content, so using the content posted on other blogs and news outlets will reduce your burden. There is nothing wrong with sharing the content of others as long as it is content that is in line with your strategy. Also, don't be afraid to reshare old content of your own that people may have forgotten about or things you posted before you had a lot of followers. It is all about showcasing your brand by staying on the top of the minds of your consumers. Any good content you share will be instrumental in helping you accomplish this goal.

At the end of the day your main goal is to eventually capitalize off of your brand in some way, so at some point you have to ask your audience to do something in order to keep the engagement going. This can start with asking them for their comments on a post, to like or follow something, to enter a contest, or lastly, to make an actual purchase of your product or service. Although we may indirectly ask for something with every post, calls to action have a direct action they are requesting of the reader, and for them to be effective, there has to be a time limit placed on the action. A great example of this would be a major university using social media to ask its students to post a photo in the school colors which might be shown at the homecoming football game on the big screen. The above-mentioned post directly asks you to do something within a window of time, and your reward for completing this action is that your picture may be shown during the homecoming football game. A post like this helps the university gain a database of students showing school pride, that they can use in future brochures and marketing materials. Everybody gets something from this call-to-action post.

TEST YOUR STRATEGY

It can sometimes be difficult to fully understand in advance what social media post will drive your audience to take any sort of action. It can be beneficial to your brand to conduct a series of tests in order to determine the best way to convert consumers into customers using social media. Many professionals in the social media marketing field utilize what's called an A/B test, which involves testing different things against one another to isolate the thing that drives people to take action on your posts, such as giving likes, clicking, purchasing, visiting the website, etc. What this means is you want to conduct an experiment to find the best combination of three main things:
1. The image used in the post
2. The text or words contained within the post
3. The time of day you post

In order to find the best combination, you have to keep some things the same while changing the others. For instance, if you're trying to determine the best image for a social media post, you would upload two to three posts using different images, but keep the wording consistent and post them both at the same time of day. After a couple days of testing, you will have an understanding of which image your audience likes the best. Now you can conduct another test on which text or wording drives higher engagement, using the same process. You upload two to three posts using different text or wording but keep the images consistent and post them both at the same time of day. Once again, after a couple days of testing, you will have an understanding of which text or wording your audience likes the best. You could then go a step further by repeating the process to determine the best time of day or even day of the week for posting as well. The options are endless. The purpose of doing an A/B test is to make an educated decision on which content post will work best for building your brand's image using social media. It is your job to constantly find the best ways to communicate who your brand is to the people that have chosen to invest their time and resources into your brand.

This is why A/B testing will be a continuous process that your business will use to find ways to keep your audience captivated. Now that you have learned all these great strategies for content posting, it is imperative that you do not just set it all up and then walk away. You must do your job as a leader of an organization, which involves analyzing and measuring the results of your content posting efforts. Some brands fail by not tracking the return on investment being generated, meaning how much money they made that is directly related to your social media posting efforts. All you need to do is just log in to your social media accounts to monitor the daily traffic increases or decreases. You should also monitor your own website analytics to determine how your website traffic is changing as a result of your superb social media content posting. By analyzing these things, it will further help you in the brand- building process as we move forward on your journey toward success.

STEP 3: CREATE CHECKLIST

- ☐ SOCIAL MEDIA PAGE LAYOUT
- ☐ CONTENT POSTING
    - ☐ The Top-Down Approach
    - ☐ The 80-20 Approach
    - ☐ The Rule of Thirds Approach
- ☐ DEVELOP A SOCIAL MEDIA POSTING CALENDAR
- ☐ CREDIBILITY POST
- ☐ POST REGULARLY AND BUILD RELATIONSHIPS
- ☐ MAKE PEOPLE WANT TO FOLLOW YOU
- ☐ TARGETING YOUR AUDIENCE
- ☐ TEST YOUR STRATEGY

BY CHRISTOPH DYER

STEP 4: DOMINATE

Digital marketing is a complex new area of advertising which allows a business of any size to effectively saturate the consumers in a pre-specified geographic area with a variety of ads that can be delivered to the consumer through social media sites, mobile-apps, games, web browsing on millions of sites, and much more. The impact of digital marketing on your business profits can be astounding, if done correctly. Your business can dominate the marketplace just like the major brands but without the hefty advertising budget those big brands spend. This is because digital marketing allows you to directly target only the people you want to reach based on the way you set up the campaign. For instance, you can specifically select consumers that only live within driving or walking distance of your business location, unlike with a traditional marketing campaign. Traditional marketing on radio, newspaper, or television only allows you the option to blast your message out to anyone within their entire coverage area, with limited ability to segment the marketplace beyond a multi-zip-code area.

People often become confused about exactly what digital marketing is as well as how to successfully utilize it to market their brand. Data-driven marketing is the simplest term that best answers the question of what digital marketing is. Both are umbrella terms that simply refer to marketing your brand using the Internet or any other digital asset, such as mobile phones, tablets, etc. There are several digital marketing techniques that you can utilize in order to dominate the market while promoting your business to thousands if not millions of consumers.

Techniques such as social media marketing, search engine marketing, and digital display advertising are some of the concepts we will dive into within this chapter. While there are several other digital marketing techniques used in the market today, we believe social media marketing, search engine marketing, and digital display advertising tend to yield the best results for growing brands that desire results while being budget conscious.

The development of digital marketing began in 1990 with the creation of the first search engine, called Archie, created by Alan Emtage, then a postgraduate student at McGill University in Montreal, and Bill Heelan. This led to the first clickable banner ad in 1993, and soon after that Yahoo was launched in 1994. However, it was not until 1998 that Yahoo launched its first web search platform. That same year, in 1998, Google launched into the market with a simplified search platform free of the clutter of ads on the homepage. The advertisers on this platform would pay Google to appear in designated places within the search engine results page, which was less intrusive to the consumer and led to what is now the pay- per-click advertising model. Social media marketing is the latest innovation.

It allows a brand to advertise to a consumer based on the distinct demographic profile contained within the user's social media page. These targeted ads will appear in the regular newsfeed, so they blend in as the user scrolls. This is great for your business due to the lack of guessing involved when wondering if you are reaching the right people. This differs from traditional media advertising on radio, television, and newspaper, which sends your ad out to everyone that views, which is expensive. With digital marketing, the burden is on the brand to make sure they have properly identified the target consumer they need to advertise to using social media marketing.

Overall, digital marketing has changed the way companies release their products or services by utilizing digital marketing technology to reach the consumer. Brands are now able to interact with their customers in an entirely different way than before. The consumer has also changed the way they shop, by using their digital devices instead of walking through the malls to visit the actual stores. Because of this, it is increasingly important that as a brand you have a digital marketing strategy in order to reach the consumers you need to build your brand. It is also very important that you deliver a cohesive message throughout all of your marketing efforts in order to build your brand's identity and have staying power in the market, which will grow your revenue. Some of the information in this chapter may be complex if you are new to digital marketing, but do not let it overwhelm you. Instead, take your time to understand the various ways to utilize the digital marketing concepts discussed here to further your message and better interact with your customer base. Nowadays, people spend a lot more time on the Internet than they did ten years ago. Because of this, any traditional marketing you are doing using radio or television will not be nearly as effective without pairing it with an effective digital marketing campaign. Digital marketing is all about meeting your brand's customers in the right place, at the right moment, and where they are spending the majority of their time, which is on the Internet.

DIGITAL DISPLAY ADVERTISING

As a brand, what do you think of when someone mentions digital display advertising? You may think of those ads that pop up when you're scrolling through websites on the Internet, or you may think of the ads that appear on the popular websites you visit that are mixed within the content as you scroll and swipe. These are both what the marketing industry refers to as digital display advertising, but these are not the only types of digital display ads available to market your brand. Digital display ads come in various formats, shapes, sizes, and places throughout the Internet, so it is a good idea for you to have a firm understanding of all the options that exist to assist you in promoting your business. The best thing about digital display ads is that they cost less than ten cents per ad served on average compared to a traditional print ad in your local newspaper, which can cost you thousands of dollars just for one ad.

Digital display advertising can be a highly effective tool for promoting your business online while maintaining budget efficiency. These ads help to market your brand within your local area, drive customers into your location or website, and assist you with increasing overall sales from the customers that visit your website but do not buy anything on their first visit. Digital display ads are box-shaped ads created in multiple sizes that appear in distinct places within a website, that have been reserved by the website owner for paid advertising. The goal of any digital display ad is to draw the visitor's attention in an attempt to get them to click on the ad. Once the visitor clicks on the ad, they will then be redirected to another website or landing page in order to hopefully make a purchase or bring attention to a product or service.

To help you choose the right banner ad size for your business, below (chart 4.1) I have included a list of the top digital banner ad sizes in 2017, according to Google. Note the top performers at the bottom of the list.

CHART 4.1 TOP DIGITAL BANNER AD SIZES IN 2017 ACCORDING TO A REPORT RELEASED BY GOOGLE

ACCORDING TO A REPORT RELEASED BY GOOGLE
1. 120 x 600 – skyscraper
2. 160 x 600 – wide skyscraper
3. 200 x 200 – small square
4. 250 x 250 – square
5. 300 x 250 – medium rectangle
6. 300 x 600 – half-page
7. 468 x 60 – banner
8. 728 x 90 – leader board
9. 970 x 90 – large leader board
10. 320 x 50 – mobile leader board
11. Best performers: 300 x 250, 728 x 90, 300 x 600

DIGITAL DISPLAY AD PRICING

There are three popular pricing models when it comes to digital display advertising, which are also very similar to the way social media ads are priced, which we will discuss later. Marketing professional should always be honest in telling you that the rate of consumers that actually click on digital display ads is low, but when the ads are targeted in the right way, they can be highly effective at building your brand's name and image on the Internet. Think about digital display ads like a newspaper or television ad, meaning that their purpose is to make the general public aware of your product or service but not necessarily sell the product through the ad. Below are the three basic pricing models as well as the intended outcomes of each:

COST PER THOUSAND IMPRESSIONS (CPM)

This type of digital display ad pricing is best suited for brand awareness, meaning you just want as many people as possible to see your ad. You pay for the ads based on every thousand ads displayed on the website that the consumer sees at least half of the ad (depending on ad viewability standards). CPM pricing tends to be the least expensive pricing structure for digital display advertising because it is just general awareness advertising, which also has extremely low click rates of typically less than .05 percent on average across all ad formats.

COST PER CLICK (CPC)

Is a performance-based advertising method which is ideal if your goal is to increase website traffic for your business? It is also favorable for a growing brand because you are only paying for the ad when someone clicks on it. Another great thing about CPC pricing is that you also benefit from all the free ad impressions you get from those that never click on your ad but still see it displayed on their favorite website, which creates additional brand awareness for you for free.

COST PER ACQUISITION (CPA)

This is the ideal pricing model to invest in for any brand that wants to increase product sales as well as online transactions. However, in order to make this type of campaign effective, you must first set your target CPA goal up to reach your target consumer. Your CPA goal with this type of campaign is based on how many marketing dollars you plan to invest for each product you plan to sell. Once you set your CPA goal, you can initiate a highly effective advertising campaign that should generate income. A CPA campaign will have lots of free impressions (ad views) that will make people remember your business long term, and you will also have people clicking through to your site that don't buy anything but can later be served with remarketing ads, which we will discuss later in this section.

TYPES OF DIGITAL DISPLAY ADVERTISING

There are four main types of digital display advertising available today to market your brand to consumers that are spending time on the Internet or on their mobile phones. Keep in mind that this is in no way a full list of all the options that exist, but instead a list of the best options for a growing brand.

GENERAL AWARENESS DISPLAY

These types of digital display ads are similar to a billboard on the side of the expressway which serves the purpose of getting your brand's name and products in front of as many consumers as possible. General awareness ads have no concern for whether the consumer has expressed any interest in your brand or even your type of products/services. Instead the goal is to introduce your brand to a new population of people that may have never heard of your business. Brand awareness ads that are not directly targeting any group in particular are less expensive than most of the other categories of digital display. This type of ad unit is mainly effective at increasing website visits and name searches for your brand online, and lastly, they assist in lifting your other advertising campaign results. But they are not very effective as a stand-alone form of advertising for your brand because of the general audience they are targeting, so the consumer may not see the ads as relevant and may keep scrolling past the ad.

BEHAVIORAL & DEMOGRAPHIC TARGETING

Now that you understand the basics of digital display, let's discuss a more effective way of promoting your brand by using targeted display ads. Targeted digital display ads can be split into two main categories: inventory targeting and user targeting. Inventory and user targeting refer to placing ads on specific websites based on the content, behavior, interests, actions, geography, and demographics of that website's audience. Brands that utilize this type of targeting need to first have an understanding of the behaviors and demographic groups that closely resemble your ideal consumer. Demographics refers to a specific part of a population that has shared characteristics or traits such as gender, age, parental status, education, ethnicity, income, homeowner status, recent life events (anniversary, birthday, new job, etc.), political affiliation, relationship status, and profession.

By targeting people that only have the demographic profile of your ideal customer, you increase the likelihood of that consumer clicking on your ad. For instance, if your brand offers dog-walking services, then you would target websites that offer pet products, pet product reviews, or even pet insurance. Maybe your research shows that female homeowners over the age of forty are your ideal customer, so you can then market on websites ideal for that audience. In this example your brand would become visible to the pet owners of the world that may have an interest in a new dog-walking service. So think of the type of things that may interest the people you want to do business with, and then identify those sites that support that interest to place your digital display campaign.

RETARGETING ADS

Has there ever been a time when you visited a website then shortly after seen that same company and its product as you are viewing another website, app, or game? Remarketing is what this is called, and it is one of the most powerful digital display tools available today because it allows you to re-engage the people that have already visited your brand's website. These are people that you have already done an effective job of marketing your brand to, but for whatever reason they came to your website then left without taking action or making a purchase. After you have done such a great job reaching these people, why let them leave without providing yourself another opportunity to service them? That is like being a restaurant where people walk in the door all day then immediately turn around and walk out. As a business, it is your duty to find ways to recapture the attention of your online consumer audience in order to ensure the longevity of your business.

In addition to building brand awareness, remarketing is insurance for all the other advertising you are doing everywhere else because it brings consumers back to your brand's website that "bounced," as they say in the industry, meaning the visitor left your website after viewing only one page. Remarketing ads can also make consumers feel like your brand is everywhere they are, which can make them think you are a brand that understands their needs, which will help them gain brand loyalty to your business. Visitors who are served with remarketing display ads are 70 percent more likely to return to your website and buy something versus website visitors that are not served with remarketing ads. Social media also allows you to remarket to users that have clicked on your ads, regardless if they are on their desktop, mobile phone, or app. It is a highly effective tool that every business should be using, but sadly, a great majority of growing brands do not because of the lack of understanding on how it works. Let's discuss in more detail in the next section.

HOW RETARGETING WORKS

Less than 2 percent of website traffic converts me on the first visit. Converting refers to the consumer taking any action, such as making a purchase, signing up for something, etc. Remarketing enables a brand to re-engage that 98 percent of the consumers that have left without making a purchase. Remarketing is a cookie-based technology which simply drops a JavaScript code called a pixel onto the consumer's device during the site visit. The pixel or code goes completely unnoticed by the user and in no way interrupts the website's performance if done correctly. Now that the pixel is on the user's computer or mobile device, anytime they visit a website that has display ads available for sale, the pixel will be initiated and the user will be served your ad—as long as the website is within your chosen ad network. Because ads are only served to website visitors that have your brand's pixel installed on their device, it is highly effective and targeted with pinpoint accuracy. Therefore, you are not wasting your budget serving ads to people that have never shown interest in your business, plus it increases the likelihood that the consumer will make a purchase.

BY CHRISTOPH DYER

HOW TO MAKE RETARGETING WORK

Remarketing is a great tool that every brand should be utilizing, but it must be part of a comprehensive digital strategy, or else it will not work. You must be actively marketing your business in other ways throughout the Internet in order to increase website traffic, so you can then remarket to those site visitors. Remarketing is the best tool for converting website visitors because the ads continue to follow them until you exhaust your budget or the user clears their cookies. Just make sure you are instituting the other strategies contained within this book in order to receive the maximum benefit of an effective remarketing campaign. Some people are more visual learners, so we have included a chart (4.2) which illustrates how the remarketing process works.

CHART 4.2. REMARKETING PROCESS DIAGRAM

GEO-MARKETING

A new revolution is underway in the world of digital marketing that does things brands once dreamed they could do to influence sales and brand awareness. An old phrase used mainly in commercial real estate is that the three most important elements of success for a new business are "location, location, location." Geo-marketing goes above and beyond in placing your business in the right location. It allows your growing brand to advertise directly to the potential customers that may have an interest in your business, directly on their mobile device. Geo-marketing uses a combination of cellular data, Wi-Fi data, and GPS coordinates to define the exact geographic location or boundary of the user.

Once this virtual fence is created, advertising is initiated based on these coordinates in a variety of methods. These methods may include display ads delivered by way of websites, apps, or games the consumer is viewing, as well as email alerts, text messages, or notifications coming from mobile apps, etc. Brands are now able to market directly to mobile users with location-based targeting. For instance, a sports memorabilia company could use geo-marketing to advertise directly to consumers sitting in a football stadium watching a game, while keeping ads from being shown to anyone outside of the stadium area.

This can be a great tool for creating brand awareness for any business. It drives customer traffic into your business without you having to physically advertise at every event, which can be too expensive for the average small business. The opportunities are endless for how to utilize geo-marketing, but once again, it must be part of a comprehensive marketing strategy.

HOW TO USE GEO-MARKETING

The companies best suited for using geo-marketing are virtually any business, since digital technology has made it affordable for even small companies to use. Next is a comprehensive list of the types of customers that can be targeted using geo- marketing as well as the best uses of the technology to reach these consumers in order to build your brand.

LOCAL CUSTOMERS

If you are a business that wants to drive new customers into your location, geo- marketing can assist you in doing this by sending digital display ads to clients within your local area that are within driving distance of your location. You could also utilize the technology to identify customers within your local area that have expressed interest online in products or services that you sell. Geo-marketing could also be used, for instance, to create a geo-fence around a factory area or construction site for a personal injury attorney that wants to increase awareness of his or her services to factory workers that may get injured on the job.

MOBILE DEVICE USERS

Consumers now are able to receive a variety of coupons, discounts, and other push notifications anytime through mobile apps on their phones. There is also beacon technology within grocery stores that allows the consumer to receive coupons while in store based on their shopping habits and physical location in the store. If the mobile user's phone has been in the area of a certain restaurant, the consumer may notice offers appearing online for that particular restaurant that is using geo-fence technology. The options are endless; the only limitation to geo-marketing is the budget the business has available, because this is one of the most expensive types of digital display advertising.

SOCIAL MEDIA USERS

It is very popular nowadays for consumers to "check in" to different locations using social media applications. These businesses that are checked in to are able to use this social media data to send out coupons, offers, and display ads knowing that someone has already expressed interest in the business. Social media has a variety of its own digital display options, which we will discuss in the next section so we can elaborate more on how to effectively use social media to market beyond typical posting.

SOCIAL MEDIA MARKETING

A professional social media strategy begins with having an effective plan of action. Sounds easy, right? Unfortunately, this is the major reason why so many business owners fail at being effective at using social media. Without a plan, you run the risk of not being organized in your strategy, which can confuse prospective clients about whom or what your brand represents. Everything you do using social media networks needs to be part of a larger cohesive plan that demonstrates and exemplifies how your brand should be viewed by consumers. This should be fairly easy to put together considering you have been reading this book while developing the image you want for your brand. We will begin this section by discussing what you should include within your social media marketing strategy. If done correctly, this should make the remainder of your digital marketing efforts easier. Your goal as a business is to make a profit while limiting expenses. This is the best part of a social media marketing campaign, because it allows you to reach a lot of people with a limited investment.

Developing an effective social media marketing plan involves first doing an assessment of your current social media accounts to determine where they are now versus where you want them to be in the future. Refer back to the social media calendar you created in the previous section to guide you in this process. Also try to quantify things wherever possible, which means look at the numbers. How many followers or friends do you currently have versus where do you want that number to be six months from now? Post engagement, which refers to actions that page visitors perform on your social pages, such as make comments, share, and give likes to the things you post. Your goal is to increase post engagement as a part of your marketing campaigns on social media because it will only help to increase awareness of your brand. Your social media marketing plan should also include which social media sites best reach your target consumer and the types of ads available on those sites. Your plan should also focus on a specific period of time of less than six months, given the fact that things change so rapidly in digital marketing, and you will want to update your strategy monthly.

The following chart (4.3) lists all of the ad types available on social media:

CHART 4.3. FACEBOOK & INSTAGRAM AD TYPES 2018

AD TYPES 2018
• Facebook feed ads
• Facebook carousel ads
• Facebook right column ads
• Facebook in-stream video ads
• Facebook instant articles ads
• Facebook marketplace ads
• Audience network native, banner and interest ads
• Sponsored message ads
• Messenger home ads
• Facebook collection ads (including canvas)

A necessary component in the goal- setting process is to determine how you will track the success of your social media marketing strategy. In addition to the obvious things such as likes, comments, shares, and re-tweets, make sure you pay attention to what really matters to your business, which are the leads generated, referrals that came from social media, and the overall conversion rate of those leads. Conversion rate refers to the percentage of user who take a desired action that you want, such as a making a phone call to your business, making a purchase online, or completing a form on your website.

It is the job of your individual brand to determine what you count as a converting lead, based on what you need more of or just based on the way your brand does business. If you have an e-commerce business, your main conversion factor may be clicks that turn into sales of products on your website. Whereas a software company may care more about ad clicks that lead to a software download or a form being completed on the website. Take the time to determine what you want more of before starting this campaign.

Once you determine what the conversion factor will be, simply take the total number of conversions you are currently receiving and then divide that by the total number of ad clicks you are currently receiving, and that will give you your conversion rate. For example, if your brand had 100 conversions from 1,000 clicks on a post, your conversion rate would be 10%, since $100 \div 1,000 = 0.1$ or 10%.

Why does your conversion rate matter, you ask? The conversion rate is the biggest indicator you have as a brand to let you know if your marketing efforts are working. It also provides you with insight into what parts of your campaign are working better than others, so you can make adjustments accordingly. The purpose of this book is not just to tell you when and where to market your brand, but to provide you with a road map of how to advertise that brand in the most efficient way possible without wasting tons of money along the way. Therefore, you must also set proper benchmarks within your plan of what success would look like to you once achieved, based on the industry you are in.

The term benchmark refers to a set of standards which are used as a reference point for evaluating the quality or performance of your advertising campaigns. Benchmarks may be based on the past experiences of your business or the performance of other firms within your industry, but observing benchmarks allows you to monitor your progress along the way so you can adjust your strategy as time goes on, which will keep your brand on top of the minds of your prospective consumers.

The major benchmarks that every brand should look at with all of their digital marketing activities are: average click- through rate (CTR) by industry, average cost per click (CPC) by industry, average conversion rate (CVR) by industry, and average cost per action (CPA) by industry. You can look up these benchmarks on the Internet for your industry. Looking at benchmarks by industry is extremely important because each industry may have a different conversion goal in mind, so it would be misleading to look at the average click-through rate for a travel agent versus a personal injury attorney, for instance, because they have totally different ways in which they may want to convert clicks into leads.

To the personal injury attorney, a conversion may be someone completing a consultation request form, whereas the travel agent may count a conversion as someone that pays for a vacation package onsite after clicking on the initial social media ad. Both have a desire to convert clicks into conversions, but in two distinctly different ways that would not be applicable to each other's business.

As we talked about earlier your brand should always use the SMART format of setting your goals. Each business goal you have should be specific, measurable, attainable, relevant, and time based, including your goals for your marketing efforts. For instance, a company may set a SMART marketing goal by stating, "We will post videos three times a day on all our social media sites, showcasing our new product line. Our target is to gain twenty likes and three comments per post during the month of May." Having an effective plan of action for your business will provide you with the greatest opportunity for success in a world full of other companies competing for the same consumers' attention.

GAIN INSIGHT FROM YOUR FOLLOWERS

A great way to understand how you should market to your potential consumer audience is to scroll through the social media pages of people that resemble your target customer. Observe the types of content they share on their pages amongst friends and family, in order to gain more knowledge on the type of things your brand should be doing to engage them. Also look at their writing style within the captions on posts so your brand understands how to effectively communicate to that audience.

Many major brands struggle with understanding the consumer audience they are attempting to market toward, which leads to money being wasted on marketing that is ineffective at reaching the right people. By understanding the ways in which your potential customers communicate with others within their peer group, you can be more effective at speaking the language and words that will move them to take action. We all know of countless retailers that failed to understand who we were as consumers as well as how to communicate to us, which has led many of those retailers to bankruptcy.

That will not be the fate of your brand, because you will do your homework to understand what inspires your audience, using the information contained within the social media profiles of others. It is also a good idea to understand the habits of your audience on social media prior to starting your marketing campaign, because you want to know why they share the things they choose to share with their friends as it relates to your business.

Some people post things that are related to a cause or issue that the community they represent cares about, while others may post about things that are new and innovative that people need to be made aware of. Understanding both how and why your audience communicates using social media will assist you in crafting engaging advertising content that will connect the dots in the brains of your consumers by addressing some need they have in their life for your brand's products.

Looking at your competitor's ads on social media is always suggested, not only to see what they are great at, but also to see what they are really bad at doing. This will allow your brand to find that niche in the market that is not being served by the current brands out there, which is what is needed to be successful. If your brand is not doing anything different than the competition, then your business will not be around for very long. Do your research on your audience so you can make your advertising stand out from everything else. This will lead to lots of engagement.

SOCIAL MEDIA ADVERTISING PRICING

There are four popular pricing models when it comes to social media digital display advertising:

COST PER THOUSAND IMPRESSIONS (CPM)

With this pricing option your brand will pay a set rate every time your ad is served to one thousand users.

COST PER CLICK (CPC)

This performance-based advertising method is ideal if your goal is to increase website clicks and product sales. CPC pricing is also great because of all the free ad impressions you get from the people that see your ad displayed on the Internet without clicking on the ad.

COST PER ACTION (CPA)

CPA ad pricing is only available when you choose the option "Website Conversions" as your "Ad result" in the Ad creator on Facebook.com. This pricing option allows you to only pay when someone clicks on your ad. This is an ideal pricing model for your business if your goal is to increase sales of products or services. However, keep in mind that for this to be effective, you have to define who your target social media user is in order to get quality clicks from likely buyers. You will also gain lots of free impressions from the clients that see your ad but do not click on it, which allows you to further your brand name without having to pay for the impressions.

COST PER LIKE (CPL)

This pricing model allows a business to track how much is spent to get social media users to "like" your Facebook page after clicking your ad.

SOCIAL MEDIA AD TARGETING STRATEGIES

There are a number of ways to target users on social media which will expose your brand to thousands of users that you can promote your business to. To learn how to effectively target users, please review chart 4.4 below. Each of the strategies refers to the ways in which Facebook allows you to target its users based on various behaviors. The strategies are different depending on what type of results your company is trying to achieve.

Compare each strategy to your personal business strategy in order to ensure you are reaching your goals by using the best targeting method for your brand. Also make sure to review the current strategies available on Facebook and the other social media sites, as social media sites adjust their policies rapidly, and some that are included here may already be outdated.

Use the listed strategies as a way to understand what your options are. If a platform does not allow you to choose one of the listed strategies or if you have any trouble, simple contact them to request further assistance. Selling advertising to companies is the main way most social media sites make money, so they are more than happy to walk you through every aspect of how to implement your advertising campaign and target the correct users on their website.

Chart 4.4. Facebook Ad Targeting Strategies for 2018

DEMOGRAPHICS	BEHAVIORS
Location Age Gender Languages Relationship Status Education Work Financial Status Home Generation Ethnic Affinity Parents Life Events Politics (US)	Behaviors Automotive Business-to-Business Charitable Donations Digital Activities Expatriates Financial Job Role Media Mobile Device User Purchase Behavior Travel Residential Profiles Seasonal & Events
INTEREST	**CONNECTIONS**
Business & Industry Entertainment Family & Relationships Fitness & Wellness Food & Drink Hobbies & Activities Shopping & Fashion Sports & Outdoors Technology	Target people that have specifics connections to your brand's pages, events, or app. Limit your ads to only be served to people with some type of connection to your business. They must also meet certain other criteria that you select during the campaign setup. **Remarketing** people who have visited your website Custom phone number list Custom facebook list of user ids

SEARCH ENGINE MARKETING (SEM)

In today's fast-paced digital world, there are millions of companies trying to get the same customers' attention that you are on a daily basis. Because of this, search engine marketing (SEM) has become an effective way to grow your brand in this competitive business environment we are currently in. Consumers are constantly using their mobile devices, computers, and tablets to search for various products or services to solve whatever problem they have.

This is where search engine marketing (SEM) plays a key role in helping your business grow by advertising your brand within the results pages of millions of online web searches. Users have multiple search engines to choose from, which provides you with a variety of options to promote your brand using Google, Yahoo, Bing, or any of the various other search engines and online directories.

Search engine marketing (SEM) is the process of using paid advertisements on Internet search engines to market your brand. These paid advertisements will appear within the search engine results page in specific pre-determined places depending on various factors. This section will provide you with an overview of what SEM is in order to help you to expand your business using the Internet. If you have ever searched for anything online, this process should make sense in connecting how your business can use SEM to create additional revenue. The process begins when a consumer uses a popular search engine or directory to initiate an online search for a product such as "local pizza restaurant." Within seconds the search engine provides the user with a list of results called a search engine results page (SERP), which also may contain text ads in the sponsored sections of the page.

If the user decides to click on one of the sponsored ads, they will be redirected to the sponsoring company's website where they can do more research. The consumer then may decide to make a purchase, contact the business, or leave the website. The local pizza restaurant in this example would be charged for the one click from the text ad which resulted in the consumer being redirected to the restaurant's website. If the consumer clicks through to the restaurant's website then instantly leaves without making a purchase, the restaurant is still billed for the click. This is why it was stated earlier that remarketing is insurance for your other ad campaigns, because it attempts to bring the consumer back to your website after their initial visit.

The graphic below provides a simple visual guide to show you how the process of SEM works.

CHART 4.5. HOW SEARCH ENGINE MARKETING WORKS

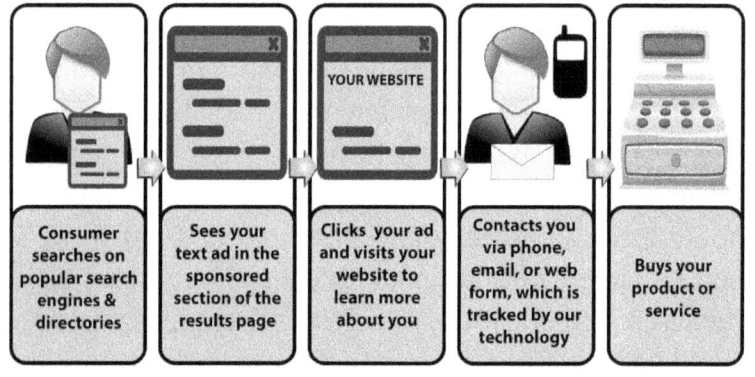

KEYWORDS

Search engine marketing allows you to advertise your brand to consumers that are highly motivated to buy at the exact moment of their online search. The foundation of all these searches is the keywords the consumer types into the search bar in order to find what they are looking for. As a brand, you have to research what terms someone would type into a search bar in order to find your products or services. This may seem overwhelming, but it is not. You are simply developing a list of relevant words that describe what your business does, the location it serves, the products you offer, its attributes, and well-known industry terms people may use to find what you offer in an Internet search.

Once you determine those relevant terms, simply enter them into the keyword suggestion tool of the search engines you choose to advertise on. The tool will then provide you with a list of additional words and phrases that relate to your chosen keywords that you can then use as a part of your SEM campaign.

The keyword suggestion tool should also provide you with priceless research, such as historical statistics about the number of people that have searched for these terms recently. The tool will also predict the number of clicks as well as the conversion you are expected to receive based on your bid, budget, and chosen keywords. When developing your keyword list, use terms that will help you identify the intent of the person searching, to measure the probability of them making a purchase. Certain keywords can help identify the user's intent to take action, such as "buy," "deal(s)," "sale," "coupon(s)," and "free shipping."

Separate each of your products that you are advertising into separate ad campaigns which focus exclusively on products or services that are alike. For example, if you are a personal injury lawyer, one campaign would focus on work-related injury claims, while the other campaign may focus on car accident injury claims. By doing this you target all of your keywords on things related only to that subject, instead of trying to squeeze too many subjects into one ad campaign. You could go even further by creating what is called ad groups, which are subcategories of relevant products or services. In the personal injury attorney example, one campaign could focus on different types of work-related injuries, such as slip and falls or construction site injuries. The car accident ad campaign could have separate subcategories, such as manufacturer recall-related accidents or uninsured motorist claims. By developing ad groups, you can not only reduce your advertising cost, but also increase the number of clicks from your search engine marketing campaign overall.

LANDING PAGES

One of the biggest factors that determine if your SEM campaign will be successful is the quality of your landing pages. The design and message within your landing page is something that cannot be overlooked because a poor design can lead to consumers quickly leaving your website. This would mean that all of your time, effort, and money would be wasted, which is surely not what you want. Make sure that the ad is directly related the product, service, or goal of your campaign in order to have the maximum impact on the consumer.

Once a visitor gets to your website, make sure they know what to do next, using well-designed landing pages. Clearly tell the visitor what the next step is. Regardless if that is making a purchase or completing a form, you must quickly make it clearly visible to the consumer. By prominently showing your call to action at the top of the page as discussed previously, you give your brand the biggest opportunity to capture the visitor's attention in order to motivate them to do what you want them to do. Brands always win with a simple, clean design for their landing pages, mainly because it is easier for the consumer to take in the message. So keep it simple when developing landing pages by having quality design, limited text, and visually stunning images that instantly grab the visitor's attention.

SEARCH ENGINE MARKETING PROCESS

The following outline will guide you step-by-step through the process of creating an effective search engine marketing campaign.

PHASE 1: RESEARCH PHASE

- ☐ Review your website.
- ☐ Research competitors' websites.
- ☐ Identify the location(s) where you will focus your campaign.
- ☐ Do initial keyword research.

PHASE 2: CAMPAIGN SETUP

- ☐ Perform advanced keyword research.
- ☐ Create your ad(s).
- ☐ Develop the landing page.
- ☐ Set up your Google AdWords account.

PHASE 3: DAILY CAMPAIGN MANAGEMENT & PERFORMANCE REVIEW

- ☐ Track installation and test ads.
- ☐ Launch SEM campaign.
- ☐ Monitor performance.
    - ☐ Check the number of impressions, bounce rate, and clicks.
    - ☐ Check conversion rate for ads.
- ☐ Assess the campaign.
    - ☐ Adjust the bid amount.
    - ☐ Adjust ads in an effort to gain better performance and improve clicks.
    - ☐ Adjust landing pages.
- ☐ Perform analysis and give feedback.
    - ☐ Determine the return on investment for the SEM ad campaign

CHART 4.6. SEARCH ENGINE MARKETING PROCESS

STEP 4: DOMINATE Checklist

- ☐ DIGITAL DISPLAY ADVERTISING
- ☐ DIGITAL DISPLAY AD PRICING
  - ☐ COST PER THOUSAND IMPRESSIONS (CPM)
  - ☐ COST PER CLICK (CPC)
  - ☐ COST PER ACQUISITION (CPA)
- ☐ TYPES OF DIGITAL DISPLAY ADVERTISING
  - ☐ GENERAL AWARENESS DISPLAY
  - ☐ BEHAVIORAL & DEMOGRAPHIC TARGETING
  - ☐ RETARGETING ADS
  - ☐ GEO-MARKETING
  - ☐ HOW TO USE GEO-MARKETING
    - ☐ LOCAL CUSTOMERS
    - ☐ MOBILE DEVICE USERS
    - ☐ SOCIAL MEDIA USERS
- ☐ SOCIAL MEDIA MARKETING
  - ☐ GAIN INSIGHT FROM YOUR FOLLOWERS
- ☐ SOCIAL MEDIA ADVERTISING PRICING
  - ☐ COST PER THOUSAND IMPRESSIONS (CPM)
  - ☐ COST PER CLICK (CPC)
  - ☐ COST PER ACTION (CPA)
  - ☐ COST PER LIKE (CPL)

- [ ] SOCIAL MEDIA AD TARGETING STRATEGIES
- [ ] SEARCH ENGINE MARKETING (SEM)
    - [ ] KEYWORDS
    - [ ] LANDING PAGES
- [ ] SEARCH ENGINE MARKETING PROCESS
    - [ ] PHASE 1: RESEARCH PHASE
        - [ ] Review your website.
        - [ ] Research competitors' websites.
        - [ ] Identify the location(s) where you will focus your campaign.
        - [ ] Do initial keyword research.
    - [ ] PHASE 2: CAMPAIGN SETUP
        - [ ] Perform advanced keyword research.
        - [ ] Create your ad(s).
        - [ ] Develop the landing page.
        - [ ] Set up your Google AdWords account.
    - [ ] PHASE 3: DAILY CAMPAIGN MANAGEMENT & PERFORMANCE REVIEW
    - [ ] Track installation and test ads.
    - [ ] Launch SEM campaign.
    - [ ] Monitor performance.
        - [ ] Check the number of impressions, bounce rate, and clicks.
        - [ ] Check conversion rate for ads.
    - [ ] Assess the campaign.
        - [ ] Adjust the bid amount.

- ☐ Adjust ads in an effort to gain better performance and improve clicks.
- ☐ Adjust landing pages.
- ☐ Perform analysis and give feedback.
  - ☐ Determine the return on investment for the SEM ad campaign

CONCLUSION

Congratulations, you now have a complete overview of everything you need to get your business up, running, and moving toward success. You know how to analyze your market to position yourself correctly in it, and you have made sure you are legally covered so you can launch with confidence. You have named your business and set up your online presence. You understand how to effectively market to your target audience using today's technology, and you have built your brand.

We understand that though all of this seems simple in nature, it can be a lot to take in, and even more to implement all on your own. That's why so many brands turn to business consultants in order to assist them in developing and implementing an effective marketing strategy.

With nearly 80 percent of businesses failing within their first 18 months, according to Bloomberg, it's important to have someone in your corner who has experience doing things right. This will help you navigate the uncertain startup period to grow a strong, stable business you can build on into the future.

This book has taken the guesswork out of lasting business success! Now go implement the strategies that you have just learned to build your brand, accomplish your dreams, and have many prosperous days and a happy, joyful life.

ACKNOWLEDGEMENTS

This book is dedicated to my mother Crystal Dyer, Owner of Gone Again Travel & Tours located in Chicago, IL. She has always inspired me to work hard at multiple things simultaneously. She worked for over 20 years in corporate America as a database manager for AT&T, while having several successful side ventures. She has now dedicated her life to being the best travel concierge in the industry and continues to motivate me toward greatest every day. My mother has influenced my life, career and decisions in so many positive ways.

I would like to personally thank my beautiful, energetic and loving mother for always challenging me to give my best to the world and to have a positive impact on everyone I meet. Please feel free to contact her travel agency for any of your Corporate and group travel needs at: www.GoneAgainTravel.com

BY CHRISTOPH DYER

ABOUT THE AUTHOR

After a successful career in radio and newspaper advertising, the author, Christoph T. Dyer, transitioned into digital marketing, where he become a certified expert in Google analytics and social media marketing. During his career, which spanned more than fifteen years, he worked with thousands of business clients both small and large to show them the strategies needed to successfully market their business to the public while tracking the results using digital analytics. He assisted his clients in growing their business revenue even during down times in the economy.

Christoph T. Dyer always had a desire to help others succeed, which led him to develop strategic plans for each client in order to identify the best path to successfully reach the client's desired goal. He has also created several successful companies of his own which taught him valuable lessons about how to run a business and advertise without having a million-dollar budget. He now runs a business consulting firm which helps companies improve performance and efficiency by assessing weaknesses and recommending solutions. The author has a deep passion for helping other companies and entrepreneurs, which is what inspired him to write this book containing the four steps to successfully building your idea into a profitable business.

www.ingramcontent.com/pod-product-compliance
Lightning Source LLC
Chambersburg PA
CBHW071233170426
43191CB00032B/1510